◇ LOVE ◈ ♥

the SH!T

* OUT OF ◇

YOURSELF

Because Your Life Depends On It

ZOEY ARIELLE POULSEN

For permission requests, please contact the publisher at:
Mango Publishing Group
2850 Douglas Road, 3rd Floor
Coral Gables, FL 33134 USA
info@mango.bz

For special orders, quantity sales, course adoptions and corporate
sales, please email the publisher at sales@mango.bz. For trade and
wholesale sales, please contact Ingram Publisher Services at custom-
er.service@ingramcontent.com or +1.800.509.4887.

Love the Sh!t Out Of Yourself: Because Your Life Depend On It

Library of Congress Cataloging
ISBN: (paperback) 978-1-63353-681-4, (ebook) 978-1-63353-682-1
Library of Congress Control Number: 2017906659
BISAC category code SEL021000 SELF-HELP / Motivational &
Inspirational

Printed in the United States of America

"AND, WHEN YOU
WANT SOMETHING, ALL THE
UNIVERSE CONSPIRES IN HELPING
YOU TO ACHIEVE IT."

- PAULO COELHO, THE ALCHEMIST

FOR MY
SUBSCRIBERS

"Zoey is truly the queen of positivity. She has managed to create a life she loves and thrives on, all through consistent positive thinking. She is with no doubt my number one source whenever I need an extra boost of motivation and positivity."

— KIA LINDROOS, CO-FOUNDER KIA-CHARLOTTA

"Love the Sh*t Out of your Life is bursting with positivity and joy. Zoey Poulsen gives you the essential, every day tools to transform and create the life of your dreams while simultaneously loving yourself as you are in the present moment. A must read for everyone!"

— MACKENZIE FLY, YOUTUBER

"Zoey's positive outlook is infectious, and
she has a unique talent for harnessing life's
possibilities. This book shares her secret to self-
love, self-belief and taking a leap of faith
to create a life you love."

— CHERYL (NON-STOP PARIS), YOUTUBER

"Zoey is a true inspiration. She is a constant
source of positivity and her life is a living
example that you can achieve anything you
want in this life if you truly believe in yourself
and the power of the Universe."

— ANASTASIYA GORSHKOVA, YOUTUBER

TABLE OF CONTENTS

INTRODUCTION

It is too often we over-work ourselves to please others without taking quality time to focus on ourselves and our personal well-being. Life can be a rollercoaster, but regardless of what the agenda brings for the day, week, month or year it is crucial to take part in self-love. We all need reminders now and then about how great and truly capable we are of achieving all of our dreams and desires in life. The best thing we can do to improve our state of mind is to partake in daily reminders. By harnessing the power of positive thinking we can begin to grant ourselves a happy, fulfilling life, attracting all that we yearn for. We cannot be our greatest version if we haven't served ourselves first, this book is your guide for that. It's time to **Love the Sh!t out of Yourself!**

I want this book to be your new best friend. It is here to remind you that you are pretty darn great on a daily basis for as long as it takes. I've learned to remind myself of this, and you know what? It feels pretty darn great! It is even kind of addictive in the best possible way. While this might seem like a fluffy little exercise, it runs quite deep and will serve you for the rest of your life. Are you ready to live your dream life? Well, this book is the perfect place to start.

If you find yourself feeling overwhelmed and drained by the bustling of life, it is time to stop in your tracks and do an attitude adjustment, or more specifically a "gratitude adjustment." Whenever you find yourself at an exhaustion or frustration point, recognize it, and remind yourself that you are in need of some "me TLC," a radical dose of self-care. You need to soak up the glory of your very being and feel grateful for all that you have accomplished in

life. In addition to feeling gratitude, it is time to compliment that practice with affirmations.

WHAT ARE AFFIRMATIONS AND HOW TO THEY WORK?

Affirmations are the action or process of affirming something; a powerful form of self-talk. It is important that when practicing affirmations we repeat, focus and visualize what it is we wish to receive. Affirmations help our conscious brain communicate with our subconscious brain. By using feeling-provoking words within our affirmations such as: love, happiness, abundance, etc. we are imprinting emotions. By attaching feelings to our affirmations such as "happiness" we are communicating with the subconscious brain and letting it know we enjoy the feeling of happiness and wish to attract more of it into our lives. The more we practice affirmations

the sooner our dreams and desires will come to us. It won't take long before you come to realize how powerful your mind is, and how abundant this practice can really prove to be.

HOW OFTEN SHOULD I USE THEM?

Affirmations should be as used as often as possible. Whether this be reciting them in the morning first thing when you get up, thinking them in your head while you brush your teeth or writing them out before bed, use them daily.

HOW FAST WILL THEY WORK?

Affirmations can work instantly or over a long period of time, it all depends on your focus and consistency with the practice. After dedicating yourself to your affirmations you will begin to notice the benefits such as a more positive

mindset, the attraction of specific people and events into your life and the achievement of your goals. Once you begin to notice this and are pleased with the results you will obtain a gratitude mindset. A grateful mindset is your way of letting the Universe know you are so happy to have received everything you have in life, and you are looking forward to receiving more. The more grateful you are, the faster affirmations work. So get dedicated to loving yourself and your life!

ARE YOU READY?
GO GET 'EM GOAL-DIGGER!

THE ART OF SELF-AFFIRMATION: HOW TO USE THIS BOOK

STEP ONE:

Get rid of all limiting beliefs. Limiting beliefs are those thoughts and barriers in your mind that make you believe you cannot achieve something or do not deserve something. It is time to stop sabotaging yourself. You were given this precious thing called life with this specific body and mind so it is time to become your own best friend, your own cheerleader and make this life an outrageously positive experience. You were born a star now start shining like one; literally, you're made up of atoms from exploded debris in the universe.

You're creative, infinite, intelligent and beautiful beyond measure; you're stardust.

STEP TWO:

Ask yourself, "How are you feeling today?" If the answer is positive then great this book will be a booster shot in word form! However; if you are feeling negative or have any red-flagged, limiting thoughts, you have come to the right place. You need to be the energy you wish to attract in this world, so whatever area you are feeling a lack in, pinpoint it and look to Step Three for guidance.

STEP THREE:

On the following pages you will find a pep talk followed by 10 affirmations on various subjects.

Choose a subcategory to help bring you back to a positive mind state or amplify an area in your life where you wish to achieve more.

If you're feeling spontaneous or looking for a sign, randomly open to an affirmation and let those words be your guiding thought for the day. If you are REALLY resonating to this power-thought, keep using it every day and let it become your mantra. The more you practice affirmations the sooner they will become your reality. Use these powerful words for ideas in speeches, on your bulletin board, in your email signature, or on your social media, the more you see them, *the better*. If you are getting ready to do a presentation, a sales pitch, an interview for your dream job, record a YouTube video or any other important task, this affirmation can be the wind in your sails.

Let these words inspire you, fill your body with joy and your mind with unlimited possibilities. This book will grant you the pep talk you need followed by 10 kick ass affirmations to get you feeling back to your beautiful, confident self again. If you're already feeling fabulous, let this book super-charge your day and kickstart attracting that dream life to you.

LET'S GET STARTED!

AFFIRMATIONS FOR EVERYDAY POSITIVITY

You are a badass, we already know this, but here's an extra dose of awesomeness to kickstart your day! Carry one of these positively powerful affirmations with you throughout the day and I assure you nothing can go wrong! The best part of this dose of awesomeness is that you're giving it to yourself. You are a confident, abundant, radiant being; ain't nobody gonna tell you otherwise.

I'm kickstarting my dream life today!

I am full
of beauty
inside
and out.

My future is
overflowing
with infinite
possibilities.

Today I am
ready, willing,
and able to
follow my
dreams!

I am
motivated and
energized to
achieve my
goals today.

I deserve all
of the greatest
gifts life has
to offer.

The positive outcome is always mine.

I possess
endless
potential.

I have all of
the energy
I need to
take on the
world today.

I am
consistently
inspired by
everything
around me.

AFFIRMATIONS FOR ATTRACTING A LOVING RELATIONSHIP

Are you ready to find the one? Your perfect match? Your partner in crime? Don't worry, I got you, and you got you! Start creating space in your life, mind and heart for this special person. This practice includes the physical spaces around you, for example: setting the table for two or making room in your closet for one more. The sooner you can achieve this, the sooner they will arrive. And when they arrive…Well, when you know you know.

My perfect
match is
on the way
to me.

I am attracting
my dream
partnership.

I am worthy
of the perfect
partnership.

I have more
than enough
suiters in
my life.

My soulmate is here and on their way to me.

I have space
in my life for
a significant
other.

I am
attracting
someone
who loves me
inside-out.

I am
worthy
of love.

I envision
myself
filled with
happiness
and love.

I love
myself
completely.

AFFIRMATIONS FOR A WEALTH ABUNDANT MENTALITY

Listen up! You can't attract money by thinking about your lack of it, it's time to turn that frown upside down and kick your anxieties to the curb. You are a money magnet and here are some affirmations to include in your everyday life to begin attracting financial abundance NOW!

I attract
money
effortlessly
and easily.

Money
flows to me
like a river to
the sea.

I am
financially
free.

I pay
my bills with
wonderful
ease.

I have more
than I could
possibly need
in my bank
account at
all times.

Money is on
its way to me
from places
I could never
imagine.

I make
money
every day.

I can afford
whatever my
heart desires.

Every day in
every way
my wealth is
increasing.

I receive the
abundance of
the universe.

AFFIRMATIONS FOR DATING

So you're getting back out there, way to be badass! I'm proud of you. You're not just eye candy you're a piping hot dish of soul food. Here's what you need to remember:

I am unique,
interesting
and
enchanting.

I am beautiful
inside
and out.

I engage in
positive and
inspiring
conversations.

I am classy. I
am confident.
I am fabulous.

I have a
magic spell
on me.

I am
a prize.

I am a
captivating,
force of
nature.

I am desired.

I radiate
confidence
and beauty.

I always have meaningful conversations.

AFFIRMATIONS FOR A POSITIVE WORK ENVIRONMENT

Bad days at work? We all have them: You spilt coffee on your shirt, someone embarrassed you in a meeting or you simply fell asleep in a meeting. We're human beings and accidents happen, people power trip, and hey, people work themselves too hard sometimes. Don't take it home with you. In fact, freshen up your day with these positive words before the workday even starts.

Each day
is a fresh start
to make my
dreams
a reality.

I am always
better than I
was yesterday.

Any
moment of
discomfort is
just a blip in
the radar.

I'm
a boss.

Success
is on its way
to me.

I attract
success
every day.

No matter
what happens
I always
redeem
myself.

I am
powerful and
productive.

A wonderful
promotion
is on its way
to me.

I am
unstoppable.

AFFIRMATIONS TO ATTRACT MEANINGFUL FRIENDSHIPS

Feeling a lack of positive, powerful and fulfilling friendships in your life? Don't worry, it just means they're on their way to you and they will arrive in divine timing. For now, remember you are whole all on your own, and an inspiring friendship is only going to lift you up even higher to your greatest potential. While your friendships are on their way to you, practice these powerful affirmations.

I attract those
into my life
who fulfill my
journey.

I attract
loving,
supportive
friendships
into my life.

My friends
support
me and I
support them.

I attract
relationships
of the highest
caliber.

I am loved
and treasured
by my friends.

I am worthy
of loving
and kind
friendships.

My life is full
of uplifting,
inspiring
friendships.

My friends
help me to
achieve my
greatest
version.

I am loved
by all and I
love all.

My friends
are true,
humble
and kind.

AFFIRMATIONS FOR BEATING PROCRASTINATION

How good does it feel to get IT done? Whether it be work, a workout or homework you need to beat that little voice in your head that's making excuses like, "I could probably create a load of laundry," or "Hey, some vegan chili would be fun to make right now!" Snap out of it. Badasses get shit done and they get it done well. Read the affirmations on the following pages then set a timer on your phone for a power hour or day; whatever you need.

I am
productive.

I attract
instant
success with
every project
I take on.

I get things
done well.

Everything
I touch turns
to gold.

This task
is easy and
enjoyable.

I always get
my work done
faster than
expected.

I am able to accomplish anything I set my mind to.

Today I
block out
distractions
and remain
committed to
my tasks.

I work
quickly and
efficiently.

I produce
work of
the highest
caliber.

AFFIRMATIONS FOR ACHIEVING SPECIFIC GOALS

Alright goal-digger, it's time to achieve! Know you are so capable of achieving whatever it is your heart desires: a vacation, a promotion, a new car - you got this. Get your intentions ready, set, GO!

I visualize the
achievement
of my
goals daily.

I accomplish
everything
I set out to do.

Unseen forces
come into
play to help
me achieve
my goals.

Each day
I am steps
closer to
my goal.

My goals
and I are
one and
the same.

I am
committed
to doing
whatever it
takes to reach
my goals.

Every
obstacle
is leading me
closer to
my goal.

My goals
will be
achieved
in divine
timing.

Those around
me support
my goals
and help me
bring them to
fruition.

I achieve
every goal
I set my
mind to.

AFFIRMATIONS FOR ACHIEVING YOUR DREAM LIFE

It's not the destination we're seeking, it's the journey. Make sure your journey is a memorable, dreamy one, overflowing with radiance and beauty. These words are here for you to affirm your worthiness of receiving an upbeat, adventurous and crazy-happy life.

Each day my
dreams are
coming closer
to fruition.

I live my
dream life.

Whatever
I desire I
can acquire.

If I can see it
in my mind I
can hold it in
my hands.

My dreams
never give up
on me and I
never give up
on them!

Any doubts
become
shadows in the
sunlight of my
determination.

I believe in
myself and
I believe in
my goals.

I enjoy
taking action
to make my
dreams my
reality.

I am easily
able to find
any resources
I require
to achieve
my goals.

The more I
think about
my dreams
the faster
they become
a reality.

CONCLUSION

This is your life, only you can truly control your choices, and choosing happiness is the finest way to live life. Affirm yourself daily on the subjects you need to receive a confidence boost in or improve on and you will cultivate more and more positive thoughts throughout the day. When you have dedicated yourself to this practice everything around you will begin to fall into perfect place. Noticeable synchronicities and serendipitous coincidences will soon enlighten your life on a daily basis.

Don't wait and don't slack off. Take control of your life now. Ditch the negative self-talk, the belittling friendships and the negative environments around you. Become more and more of the radiant being you came to

the world to be, and strive for a better you, each and every day. Overflow with infectious, positive energy and harness the power of your thoughts to always work in your favor. You owe it to yourself to love the shit out of yourself every day because that's who you'll be spending the rest of your life with. Work towards creating your dream life and if you're already there then this is your sign to push yourself to achieve and attract more than you could ever possibly imagine. There is no glass ceiling, so affirm yourself of your radiance and your dreams every. single. day.

The future is infinite and so are you!

VOLARE,
ZO

ACKNOWLEDGEMENTS

Thank you to the Mango Publishing Team for bringing my dreams to a reality. Many thanks to my friends and family for inspiring my journey and of course, to my subscribers who always grant me a burst of positivity. This book would not be possible without any and all of you!

Infinite gratitude,

ZOEY

AUTHOR BIO

Zoey Arielle Poulsen, better known by her wildly popular YouTube channel: Zoey Arielle, is a 25-year-old Canadian girl living life the way it was meant to be lived. Currently working remotely in Rome, Italy. Zoey was born and raised on Vancouver Island, BC, Canada and relocated to Toronto to pursue a post-graduate degree and career in Sport & Event Marketing, where she spent a few enjoyable, transformational years. Zoey felt alive in the big city of Toronto, yet noticed time seemed to escape her as she spent the majority of her time sitting in a desk. Her zest for life and willingness to take chances, drove her to follow her dreams of living in Rome, Italy. Zoey now lives a life well-travelled and shares her positive message with the world through her YouTube channel and books. By sharing her voice and vulnerabilities with the world, she's become the digital nomad of sorts we've all come to love.

Thank you for reading.

In writing *Love the Sh!t Out of Yourself*, Zoey Arielle Poulsen did her very best to produce the most accurate, well-written and mistake-free book. Yet, as with all things human (and certainly with books), mistakes are inevitable. Despite Zoey's and the publisher's best efforts at proofreading and editing, some number of errors will emerge as the book is read by more and more people.

We ask for your help in producing a more perfect book by sending us any errors you discover at errata@mango.bz. We will strive to correct these errors in future editions of this book. Thank you in advance for your help.